Angel Aura Crystal:

"The Universe Speaks"

S.S.S. Short stories from short people for short attention spans

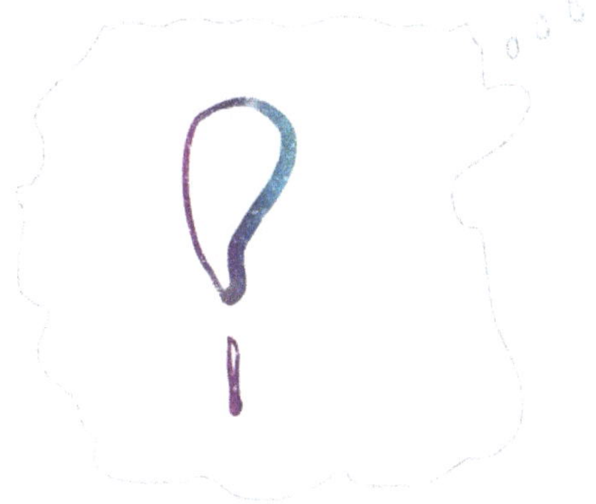

Suzanne Jansen BA, LMT, NCBTMB, CST
Ayurveda Yoga Specialist, Usui Reiki Master
Bodyworker and Spiritual Healer

Published by David McKay Publication

First Edition

Printed in the United States of America.

ISBN: 979-8-90321-012-1 (eBook)

ISBN: 979-8-90321-011-4 (Paperback)

For permissions, media inquiries, or bulk purchase information, please contact:

info@davidmckaypublication.com

Dedication

- ❖ I give thanks and dedicate this book to all the random strangers in my life who made the tiny effort to lift me up with their kindness when I needed it most. These are the people who quietly, consistently help others through their words, actions, and simple gestures of kindness: May more of us feel the inner nudge of the Universe and its unconditional love, compassion, and peace it desires for us all. All we need to do is slow down and listen.

- ❖ To our guides, angels on earth and in heaven, we are thankful for your silent protection and gentle guidance. May we have better ears to listen. Amen.

- ❖ "It takes a village." To all the surrogate families who took in my daughter and me as their own, I send my deepest gratitude.

- ❖ To the little old ladies who drove 90 miles to rescue me from creative purgatory, you lit the fire under me again. Thank you, I needed that.

Acknowledgment

For mentors, friends, family near and far, and respected colleagues, I acknowledge your presence in my life and your own personal story.

I would also like to acknowledge Stella Jay Brown and the Jay Team. This team building and belonging early on in my career was a wonderful safety net. Stella used to always say to me with a heavy British accent, "Kathy, pick yourself up from your bootstraps and get on with it!" Those words, although tough, kept me going for years on my own. Her love was tough love, which I cherish.

I will also acknowledge my own business clientele of 25 years, Riverfront Therapy Inc., Spirit of the River Yoga and Bodywork, as I learned so much from all of you.

To my daughter, Cornelia. You are gifted, beautiful, and loving. I look forward to all the talents you will offer this world with your strong heart.

Lastly, to my mother, who gave birth to me, Sue Ann Jansen (February 1948–1987); you were taken from our family and from this Earth too soon. Without a mother, I had to learn life lessons that are of immense value, despite the pain in my own journey from healing into wisdom.

This is a portrait my daughter made for me when she was a 12-year-old.

I did not know she was painting this portrait for me, so when she handed it to me and said, "Here, Mom, this is for you."

I was surprised at the green tears down my face, so I asked her what the tears meant.

She replied without missing a beat, *"Those are the tears of your soul crying for worries of the world and Mother Nature"* Green is my favorite color, so that's why they are green. In real time, I am in awe at the depth with which she saw my soul.

Yet I also felt a bit saddened that this is how she saw me, thinking, "Am I too sad all the time?"

For me, as a mother, this felt like a pretty big wakeup call. Her intentions were innocent, and yet this struck a chord in me, reminding me of a story I heard in India.

It is a story about 'The Tears of Shiva,' and how they went into the hillside where the famous Bodhi tree is to this day. Shiva cried for the worries of the world from a mountaintop, and his tears touched the Earth; the Bodhi tree sprouted. The sacred tree bore fruit which contained the Rudraksha seeds. These seeds hold the Prana, the life force of Shiva.

Tears can carry lifeforce, and I have cried many times for this Earth and its wildlife. My daughter is clear on this about her mom.

I remain in awe of her talent and appreciate this beautiful painting, which reveals her wisdom at such an early age.

Introduction by the Author.

I was born in 1972 in Orange County Hospital, Santa Ana, California, to a military family. My mother met my Marine Corps father in Los Angeles; however, we left when my older brother and I were still quite young. My mother felt LA was a dangerous place to raise kids, as she graduated from Santa Ana High School in '1964.

Since my father was from Wisconsin, they found jobs in the Midwest, close to family and a corporate hub-to-be. Raised in the suburbs of Minneapolis, MN, in the '80s, I was in the "Land of 10,000 Lakes," where we lived close to Lake Minnetonka.

When I was eleven, our family's world turned upside down. Our talented, thoughtful, hard-working mother, our matriarch, just thirty-seven years old, was suddenly in a grand mal seizure in her sleep. The next day, she was diagnosed with a malignant brain tumor; the doctors told us that she had "zero to five years to live." We will save that story about losing my childhood, the oppression, and the time it has taken to reclaim my heart and soul for another time.

I coveted my early memories alone with my mom. Sometime in my early development, I remember the moment my mother discovered I was dyslexic.

We were driving down Minnetonka Boulevard on a curve, and she asked me what the speed limit sign said. I quickly answered, "Fifty-three." Obviously, it was a 35-mph speed limit sign.

My mother did not correct me at that time. She seemed to want to ignore my dyslexia.

A) The educators had already told her an inaccurate statement from the '70s about how I was not growing fast enough on the growth chart.

B) They speculated my brain must not be developing as fast as the other children's and suggested she hold me back in school.

My mom chose to ignore them both. As I recall, she thought that was absurd and let me sort it out on my own.

Granted, I performed below average in grammar school and not much better in middle or high school, partially due to the lack of understanding of these conditions at that time.

What is interesting to me is that this memory is something my brain kept all these years. Somehow, I knew at that moment I was different. I took on this subtle awareness that something was "wrong" with me.

The effort to adapt to the normal education system was a battle for me. It was not until college and massage school that I was able to excel in academics.

Knowing now what we do about these conditions, it is no surprise that I talked too much in school and was a terrible student. I was so "bad" that I recall one teacher getting so frustrated with me that he picked up my desk and threw it over.

As pharmaceuticals take over the problem now, I would like the public to know you can work through these things naturally. It is important to recognize that one does not get rid of these brain patterns as an adult.

It is also important to understand that there are different degrees to which these conditions can vary. Today, my dyslexia and attention challenges show up only when my brain is tired. I still have attention issues, but now I understand how to cope with that spinning-out feeling. Yoga has anchored me, given me a channel, as well as just taking care of my basic health.

Blossoming fully into my gifts for healing did not start until a career change at 29 years of age.

My point is this: anyone can write, even if learning challenges are present. Now is the time for your voice to be heard; channel your own experiences into healing experiences through whichever creative expression you desire, whether it is, in fact, writing or some other expression... The time for creativity is now!

Sharing writing again at 53 feels daring, when truthfully, I have not written in 26 years. This brings me back in memory to a paper I wrote in college: my root desire—to know the human body–mind complex.

The paper I submitted for an "A" called "Mind to Body through the Arts". Even in my early twenties, I desired to write out my thoughts. However, my body chose the physical before the mental merged into balance and understanding of Self, the real purpose of yoga studies.

I learned yoga as an elective in college; we all wanted the easy "A." I noticed, as I looked around the room, there was a large diversity of humans there in size, shape, color, and creed. And it was my first experience with meditation…another short story for another time. I will say that later in life, yoga saved me from spinning out as an adult after school.

For those reading this who can relate to learning or attention issues as adults, or from a parent perspective, please check out this amazing book that changed my life around how I learn and why I have had blocks with learning.

This book from the '80s, called Smart Moves, Why Learning Is Not All in Your Head," is by neurophysiologist and educator, Dr. Carla Hannaford. It looks into the kinesiology techniques in the BrainGym™ book to help adults, elders, and children develop better balance and kinesthetic awareness lacking in today's technology-driven world.

Smart Moves is a book about how children develop and how our brain hemispheric dominance has an impact on the types of topics where our brains will excel. More deeply, I wonder why the wisdom of this book is no longer utilized in today's education system. It may not be so difficult to see why families are choosing to homeschool their children.

The feedback I hear from parents who do this expresses joy about the process, a more organically flowing way in which each child in this model has the opportunity to learn, absorb, and retain information in a nervous system that is already being taxed. I believe, from experience, kids with sensory issues are rooted in our nervous systems hijacked with fear, violence as a norm on TV, social media, in person at schools, and on the roadways. For me, as an empath, all of it is just baffling.

I am here to bring support to those who can relate and are afraid to write or create because someone may have stifled their natural abilities to learn in ways that are not the norm. Not only was I horrible at school, but there was a doll called "Chatty Cathy" introduced in 1961; coincidentally, my nickname is Kathy. And yes, in every yearbook in elementary school and middle school, my teachers wrote, *"talks too much in class," "easily distracted, a real chatty Kathy."*

Prologue

Original art gifted to us by our tall friends Angela, Ava, Zoe, and Christian. The scratch across this painting happened during the peak of the storm of our life- category five, Hurricane Michael. Short story shorter, my daughter's window broke when the room imploded, creating a suction that slung debris throughout her room, somehow this painting survived with a tiny scratch.

"Short people got no reason" ~ a song by Randy Newman that was just as off-putting as its title.

I want to start off this story with a short snippet of my playful personality.

This is how I have fun in public, or when I meet a tall person, I am about to massage.

Scenario 1: A tall person is standing next to you; you're at a grocery store… You know you need to reach something high that they can reach, so go ahead—just engage and say, "Hey, do you mind getting this thing up here?" And then offer to get them something down low, and they will inevitably laugh every time. This is a simple way to break the ice with the public and get what you need at the grocery store.

Scenario 2: My massage practice can be awkward. I'm just 5 feet 2 inches tall, and my clients often walk in at 6 feet 4 inches, it is a bit comical to have a tiny person manhandling you on a massage table. Instead of telling them their posture is horrible, I say to them, "I know that you are subconsciously apologizing for being tall around shorter people, and I give you permission not to do that." They immediately acknowledge with a smile, and their eyes recognize that I have expressed a truth rarely said aloud. I continue to tell them, "There is no need to hunch your shoulders forward for me, as I am okay with being short." "You can simply get the things up high for me, and I can get those things down low for you," and again, we laugh together.

Diversity is the key to life itself. We have a responsibility to enjoy our God-given talents and attributes. Tall, short, big, small, fatthin, brown, yellow, white, black, and anything in between is, and has been, accepted in my small, simple world.

Join me!

Bring magic back into your life by recognizing the unique gifts you were born with. Not everyone gets the chance to fulfill their greatest potential—not unless we support each other, each generation.

Through storytelling, we can share joy, laughter, and tears in our everyday lives with everyday people. Bring real-life magic back into your life through these short stories with meaningful metaphors. Give yourself permission to open yourself up and be inspired by the Universe and what it has to say to you.

Angel Aura Crystal: *an inanimate object and its journey from one owner to another.*

This is how the Universe Speaks...

A beautiful Angel Aura crystal landed at my feet in a restroom at a Tire Kingdom in Panama City, Florida. I was moving slowly, and the world was moving slower from Covid shutdowns. The year was bare bones for income; as a massage therapist, I had little other than the stimulus check. Money was tight; however, there were certain necessities you had to buy regardless of what was happening in the economy, and tires were one of them.

The commute was ninety miles along the Gulf coast. After a long, stressful series of abusive relationships, I felt like a zombie at the end of my rope. The "friend" who said he was helping me get out of the first one, in short, ended up a squatter in my house during those shutdowns, and would not leave. It got violent. Five 911 calls later, I locked him out for two days in the dead of August in fear for our safety. Finally, two court dates, a no trespassing order, and a no contact order, anyone would feel drained of all life force.

During the drive, relief from the reality of my escape from this dark cloud and manipulation started to kick in. Single mom, seven-year-old daughter, four pets. Granted, living in beach communities, it was an easy place to be a target for beach bums and addicts. Additionally, we had just survived the biggest storm of our lives: Hurricane Michael.

What I thought was going to be an ability to communicate... I experienced healing and joy through average humans in daily life. These are the gifts awaiting all of us. We just have to be open.

The setting: Imagine a hot parking lot in a North Florida beach town—23rd Street, Panama City, 6 p.m. I was their last appointment of the day; I was thankful they were open on a Saturday.

Admittedly, my face must have looked beaten down as I checked in. Thankfully, I thought, very few people were there. I was hungry, and the only thing left in the fridge was a half-eaten pack of strawberries. In my rush to revive myself, I grabbed them and tossed them into the car on my way out the door, hoping they'd sustain me...

I decided to walk back outside for fresh air, sunshine, and a light snack to help me get grounded since I was last in line. I was sitting on a concrete block in the parking lot, shoving whatever strawberries were left into my mouth, grateful for their juices. I was present and fully aware, awakening from a bad dream is what I wanted to believe.

As I felt the warm sun hitting the fatigue over my face, I felt its power—the sun, the fruit, drinking water, and the relief that I was slowly bringing myself into balance.

These few moments felt like slow motion as I sank into a place of intense gratitude for liberation from these back-to-back horrific relationships. I was bravely able to get away from the verbal lashing, slaps, and shoves without losing my life to abuse or involving my daughter.

Every parent has good and bad experiences; the important thing is to learn from them to prevent history from repeating itself. I felt I had finally won the battle to reclaim my home as mine and sovereignty over my soul; nonetheless, I felt beaten down. This time outside allowed a brief but solid release. My eyes could see again as I re-entered the Tire Kingdom. Feeling renewed by this meditation, I walked into the restrooms.

This is where I found an Angel Aura crystal. I almost thought it was a child's toy on the floor the minute I walked in. However, this was no ordinary crystal nor a toy. As I sat down, I started to realize this was something unique.

This crystal on this day, time, and place MUST be a message from the Divine. I looked again in disbelief, as surely my tired eyes were playing tricks on me. Nope—this was real. I was comically half-naked on a toilet in a public place, and when I finally accepted it, I did see a legitimate crystal lying on the floor in front of me.

In the next nanosecond, I heard: "Don't touch it; wash your hands and return it to its rightful owner."

I cleaned myself, washed my hands, and picked up the crystal to inspect it further. There was no chain, just a crystal with a molded metal top, a loop for the chain, and another loop of a cheaper metal. As I exited the bathroom, I intended to return it to the rightful owner. With only two women in the lobby, I went up to the first woman—the one who had been in before me— and asked, "Is this your crystal?"

She responded, "No."

Of course, my next thought was that it might belong to the cute college-age hippie couple sitting farther away. Her back was to me as I walked up. Her boyfriend saw me first, then she turned around, and I said, "Is this your crystal?"

In that nanosecond as her face turned around, I saw her eyes light up and look down at her rope. "Ah ha!"

I found the owner. With her immediate recognition of this item as hers, she looked down at her chest, surprised that it had come off and that she had not noticed it was missing. She then sent me a quick thank you and a smile. I handed it back, smiled, and then told her this must have been a divine message. I thanked her for the "sign." She thanked me for returning it. I went to sit and wait at my own table.

As it turned out, I was also the last customer to leave the building. So, as she and her boyfriend passed me, she had the crystal back on its rope, handing it to me, shesaid, "Here, I believe this crystal found you for a reason, and you should have it."

I fully understood this gesture, as it is said that crystals draw themselves to people, just as we are attracted to them.

I was wondering about how this crystal had come off in that moment in time. I considered it might have released itself, but dismissed that idea as preposterous. It must simply be a coincidence. Before she walked away, I asked what type of crystal it was, and she said, "It is called an Angel Aura crystal."

"Wow!" I thought, "An Angel came to me at the Tire Kingdom on my last thread of spirit!"

This was most definitely a divine message of love from beyond, encouraging me to continue and reassuring me that I have full support in every step I take.

I spent the rest of my time at the tire shop researching the meaning of this crystal. In gratitude, I read everything I could find.

Here is an excerpt of what I found online:

Angel Aura Quartz is a sweet, loving, and high-vibrational crystal that illuminates even the dullest of days. Beginning with the properties of its crystal companion, Clear Quartz, it gains its extra sparkle through a unique alchemical process (CVD). This scientific process is so phenomenal that it bonds gold, silver, platinum, and other materials to pure quartz, forming an intense healing energy.

After the manager checked out the other customers, he explained to me why he was taking so long, and I was the last person there for another hour.

He continued to tell me that the closest parts store was closed, so he had sent his co-worker to grab tires from another location that was 30 minutes away, and at this point, I knew it was already past closing time.

I apologized for keeping them past their time, and not missing a beat, he said, "Oh, do not you worry about us, Ms. Jansen. Do not you ever forget—you are worth it."

I almost burst into tears when he said this, because receiving the crystal was enough of a boost; I figured I was "done." I should mention that only someone who's been treated poorly over time understands the tiny gift this man and young lady gave me that day.

I mean, it sounds simple, but I just felt so much relief knowing I was valued by two complete strangers.

This is how the Universe works, if you pay attention.

I smiled, a touch of glistening in my eyes, and said, "Thank you for your kind words."

I believe that divine gifts come in threes: the man, the woman, and the crystal. I was paying attention to all these signs, and I took them very much to heart. So, I, too, thought the story was finished—but not just yet.

Can a jewel talk?

After what I am about to tell you, you may want to put this down and say, "No way!"

But I am going to say, "Yes way!"

Although this may be the end of the short story, it is not if you can hang on a little longer, because the journey of this crystal continues into my evening.

I was staying with a friend in Panama City, so I pulled up into her driveway after my tire adventure and went inside to greet her with this interesting story—especially how it "magically" came off its owner's rope. I set this crystal down on the kitchen counter and went to shower, in the same way it was handed to me, on its rope.

Moments later, I was out of the shower, walked back into the kitchen, and lo and behold, the crystal was lying off the rope again!

Puzzled by this, I asked my friend, "Did you take this crystal off the rope?"

She replied, "No, why would I? I have been in my own bath."

So, then I asked, "Did your husband grab this by chance?"

She again said, "No way. He has been outside, and why would a guy do that?"

So, I was sitting there looking at the mold and noticed an extra piece of fake metal attached to the soldered bit.

At that exact moment, my friend walked around the corner with a couple of chains and said, "Do you want one of these?"

As I was thinking, I heard this crystal object telling me it did not like that cheap rope it had been living on. I couldn't help but chuckle at the message, as if the item itself had a real personality attached to it.

I smiled because my friend had already read my mind and was walking around the corner with two sterling silver chains in her hand. When writing this in a story, I am baffled by how long it takes to explain this compared to how it went down in real time—we are talking a matter of seconds to discern these thoughts, actions, and outcomes.

The next nanosecond thought was that the crystal told me it liked the one on the right. As I was thinking this, my friend had already started handing me that one, telling me it was her grandmother's chain.

I then felt this intense feeling, like a homecoming of two separate things: the old, real sterling silver chain and the real sterling silver hook, which was originally soldered to the crystal during a bonding process called vapor deposition.

Do I know how old the crystal is? No, I did not ask the woman who gave it to me.

But I do know that when I got rid of the fake metal connector and the cheap rope and put these two better-quality items together, it felt right, and the crystal has not "fallen" off since.

I've worn this and can definitely feel its power, but it's not something to wear all the time. It's meant to be worn during specific moments of transition, offering deep spiritual support when it's needed most.

Do I believe someone else owned this jewelry and may be in the beyond?

Yes, I do.

I know you may be thinking people look too much into coincidences, but we know in today's world that there is a thing such as looking into too little.

I believe this story and more stories I have to tell prove something I never expected: inanimate objects can communicate energy and desire to be with another owner, and in turn, find their way home—whether from the previous soul who owned this or some other Angel connected to it. Frankly, I do not care either way. I was given a gift with layers of divine intertwining that I am still in awe of.

Naturally, some people assume anyone interested in crystals and their meanings is some kind of "woo-woo" type with no scientific basis for this belief. Yet, if you investigate older cultures in all areas of the continents, gems, rocks, sand, and soil have a deep place in the foundation of our planet Earth.

Now, this type of crystal is heated to an extremely high temperature and coated to look angelic in its light blue/purple iridescence, so there is human intervention to create this type. None of this information, of course, was something I knew anything about until I found myself at this location, of all places, getting a new set of tires!

Short message: If you pay attention to the little, seemingly coincidental happenings in life that perhaps divinity has set in place at the right time and right place, you align and open to your fullest potential and natural flow as a human being, evolving without pretext or expectations.

Outro

If you love hearing about these short yet divine experiences and want to hear more, please let me know. You decide for yourself after reading these events, which occurred in real time, to a real woman. Whether or not you believe the life of this story is of a divine nature is completely subjective.

My hope in writing is that you will feel the hook in your belly for more stories like this, and hopefully have a few of your own divine experiences manifest as a simple result of more awareness of the mundane message that you may be missing.

For me, a student of the subtle, this was the best little sliver I could share of how the Universe speaks to me, and I am expecting more magic to reveal itself in "divine timing."

Amid the chaos, I see magic in tiny messages; these are the winks from the Universe, and we can feel this gentle pulse if we slow down.

I must also share an additional moment of magic from the Universe that happened while I was getting in line with a publishing company.

Admittedly, I had been procrastinating publishing—a result of trauma. Recently, during a sort of midlife crisis, I reached out to an old mentor of mine. She and a friend came to have lunch with me, and as I listened to these two wise women talk about their lives—creating art and writing—I realized that I could have these things in my own life.

I thought, "I want to be like these women when I grow up."

At the end of that day, I had an errand to run about fifty miles away.

So, on my way back from running the errand, here I am on the road, using voice-to-text to communicate with my publisher about the over-the-phone payment.

In the nanosecond I paid the publisher, at that very moment, a paperback book flew out of the back of a truck and landed on the ground. Yes!

I thought, "What are the chances of that happening?"

I have seen trash fly out of trucks on coastal highways, but never a paperback book! I had a good chuckle to myself and thanked the Universe for giving me a wink—letting me know I am on the right track publishing this book.

About the Author

Suzanne Jansen, also known by her first name Kathleen or "KJ", has been called to three different career paths; however, they seem to hold one clear mission: healing through the arts. Over decades of Professional Choreographing and Acting on stage, and Entrepreneurship, it is about time to write and share some of the many amazing stories she has experienced.

There is no challenge she will not tackle, even taking on building houseboats on the Apalachicola River, a not-so-short story for another time. Building anything that seems impossible has somehow always been a hook for her, just because she could.

'She turned her can't into cans and her dreams into plans.'

Here she is enjoying the freedom of her spirit and sharing the gift in sweet simple stories anyone can relate to.

With over 20,000 hours of hands-on experience, her work integrates anatomy, energy healing, and mindful awareness to support physical relief, emotional release, and nervous system balance.

"I am experiencing magic, miracles, and many themes repeating themselves that I want to share. Through writing I am breaking free from the one-on-one nature of my practice; writing allows my true nature and light to be shared. I am aware I have been repressing my other creative abilities. I am coming out of the studio and into the world of writing. These reflections will help give light back into the world for the greater good."

Rooted in Hatha yoga since the mid-1990s, Suzanne draws on the union of body, mind, and spirit to guide her practice. She believes the body holds both stories and solutions, and with the right support, it knows how to heal itself. Through hands-on work and practical self-care tools, she empowers clients to move beyond quick fixes and reconnect with their deeper well-being.

Spirit of the River Yoga and Bodywork is her ongoing business of 25 years. The houseboat is no longer on the river; she moved it to land in 2009. (Yet another story for another time.) Her current consultations, advanced therapy and bodywork sessions are on land in Apalachicola, Florida.